LIFE-CHANGING IDEAS FROM
THE SERVICEBERRY
WORKBOOK

Eye-Opening Concepts from Robin Wall

Kimmerer's Book.

GoldenQuill Press

CONTENTS

"In a world where scarcity is the loudest story, let us remember the quiet abundance of nature — always giving, always sharing, always teaching us that true wealth lies in what we nurture together."

Chapter 1: The Gift of Abundance: Shifting from Scarcity to Reciprocity

Key Insights

- **Abundance as a Mindset**: The natural world offers a model of abundance, where resources are shared and distributed for mutual survival and growth. Serviceberry trees, for example, give their fruit generously to birds, animals, and humans alike, ensuring a cycle of reciprocity and renewal.

- **Scarcity vs. Reciprocity**: Modern economies often operate from a mindset of scarcity, rooted in competition and hoarding. This contrasts with ecological systems, which show that shared abundance leads to collective flourishing.

- **The Illusion of Self-Sufficiency**: True wealth is not measured by what we accumulate individually but by the strength and quality of our relationships. Nature thrives on interconnectedness, proving that survival depends on collaboration rather than isolation.

- **Redefining Value**: Wealth in a gift economy is not monetary but relational. The serviceberry tree illustrates this by distributing its "wealth" in a way that benefits the whole community.

- **The Power of Gratitude**: Gratitude transforms the way we perceive abundance. By recognizing and appreciating the gifts we receive—whether from nature, relationships, or opportunities—we begin to foster a mindset of giving and reciprocity.

- **Practical Application of Reciprocity**: When applied to human life, reciprocity can reshape personal relationships, community engagement, and even professional collaborations. The principle of mutual benefit fosters trust and growth in all spheres.

Reflective Exercises

Reflect on a moment when someone shared something with you selflessly. How did it impact your view of generosity?

_____

_____

_____

_____

_____

_____

_____

_____

_____

Consider your current relationships. Are there areas where you feel the balance of giving and receiving could improve? How can you address this?

_____

_____

_____

_____

_____

_____

_____

_____

_____

List three things you feel grateful for today. How can this gratitude inspire an act of reciprocity in your life?

_____

_____

_____

_____

_____

_____

_____

_____

_____

_____

Reflect on the concept of self-sufficiency. How has this belief shaped your life, and how might embracing interdependence benefit you?

_____

_____

_____

_____

_____

_____

_____

_____

_____

_____

How can the concept of shared abundance shift the
way you view your professional or financial goals?

_____

_____

_____

_____

_____

_____

_____

_____

_____

Actionable Steps

1. **Gratitude Journaling**: Start a daily gratitude journal. Each evening, write down three things you received that day—whether it's kindness from a colleague, a meal, or time in nature—and reflect on how you might reciprocate.

2. **Community Sharing**: Find one way to share your "abundance" with others this week. It could be donating items you no longer need, sharing your knowledge with a friend, or cooking a meal for someone in need.

3. **Redefine Wealth**: Create a list of what you value most in life—relationships, health, learning, etc.—and consider how you can invest more in these areas rather than material accumulation.

• • •

"Wealth is not the abundance of things, but the abundance of meaningful connections. True prosperity comes when we lift others as we rise."

— Inspired by Robin Wall Kimmerer

Chapter 2: Scarcity vs. Abundance: Transforming Our Economic Mindset

Key Insights

- **The Scarcity Trap**: Many modern economic systems and personal behaviors are built around a fear of scarcity—hoarding resources, competing for limited goods, and prioritizing individual gain. This mindset leads to stress, inequality, and environmental harm.

- **Abundance as a Natural State**: Nature operates on an abundance model, where resources like sunlight, water, and nutrients are distributed in ways that benefit ecosystems as a whole. The serviceberry tree embodies this principle, thriving by giving generously.

- **The Hoarding Fallacy**: Hoarding offers the illusion of security but isolates individuals and depletes communal resources. True resilience comes from shared abundance, where everyone has access to what they need.

- **The Role of Trust in Abundance**: Shifting to an abundance mindset requires trust in systems of reciprocity—believing that giving to others will lead to mutual benefit rather than loss.

- **Redefining Success**: In an abundance-based worldview, success is measured not by accumulation but by contribution and the health of the relationships you foster—whether with people, nature, or your community.

- **Applying Abundance in Everyday Life**: Embracing abundance means reassessing how we manage time, energy, and resources. It invites generosity, collaboration, and long-term thinking into personal and professional decisions.

Reflective Exercises

Reflect on a time when you acted from a scarcity mindset (e.g., withholding resources, avoiding collaboration). What drove your decision, and how could an abundance mindset have changed the outcome?

_____

_____

_____

_____

_____

_____

_____

_____

Think of an example where abundance in nature inspires trust and reciprocity (e.g., how trees share nutrients through fungal networks). How can you apply this lesson to your life?

_____

_____

_____

_____

_____

_____

_____

_____

_____

What personal or professional goals are rooted in scarcity thinking? How can you reframe them with an abundance mindset?

_____

_____

_____

_____

_____

_____

_____

_____

_____

Reflect on how your community fosters—or fails to foster—shared abundance. What steps can you take to encourage greater trust and collaboration?

_____

_____

_____

_____

_____

_____

_____

_____

_____

_____

In what areas of your life (e.g., relationships, finances, time management) do you feel most secure in abundance? How can you expand this mindset to other areas?

_____

_____

_____

_____

_____

_____

_____

_____

_____

_____

_____

Actionable Steps

1. **Practice Generosity**: Make a deliberate effort to share something valuable this week, whether it's knowledge, time, or resources. Notice how this impacts your relationships and mindset.

2. **Start a Trust Experiment**: Choose one area where you feel scarcity-driven (e.g., finances, collaboration, or time) and practice trusting the process—investing in others or a long-term solution rather than immediate gain.

3. **Reframe Your Success Metrics**: Identify three non-material measures of success that align

with abundance thinking, such as improved relationships, personal growth, or community impact.

"The opposite of scarcity is not abundance. It is enough—for all of us, for all time, if we share."

— Inspired by Robin Wall Kimmerer

Chapter 3: Gratitude as a Practice: Building a Culture of Thanks

Key Insights

- **The Power of Gratitude**: Gratitude shifts focus from what is lacking to what is present, fostering an awareness of abundance and interdependence. It deepens our connection to others, nature, and ourselves.

- **Gratitude in Nature**: The natural world models gratitude through reciprocal relationships. The serviceberry tree gives freely, and in turn, birds, animals, and humans ensure its survival by spreading its seeds.

- **Gratitude as Reciprocity**: Gratitude is not just a feeling but an action. When we express thanks, we acknowledge our debt to others and commit to giving back in meaningful ways.

- **Cultivating a Culture of Thanks**: Societies thrive when gratitude becomes a shared value. It fosters trust, strengthens relationships, and creates an environment of mutual respect and generosity.

- **Challenges to Gratitude**: In a fast-paced, competitive world, it's easy to take gifts for granted or overlook the interconnectedness of life. Practicing gratitude requires mindfulness and intention.

- **Applying Gratitude Beyond the Personal**: Gratitude can transform workplaces, communities, and even economies by encouraging collaboration, reducing conflict, and prioritizing shared well-being.

Reflective Exercises

Reflect on a gift you've received recently (tangible or intangible). How did it make you feel, and how did you express your gratitude for it?

_____

_____

_____

_____

_____

_____

_____

_____

_____

Think of a person who has significantly contributed to your growth or well-being. How can you show gratitude to them in a way that feels meaningful?

_____

_____

_____

_____

_____

_____

_____

_____

_____

What does gratitude mean to you beyond saying "thank you"? Reflect on how you embody gratitude in your daily actions.

_____

_____

_____

_____

_____

_____

_____

_____

_____

_____

Think of a moment when you overlooked an opportunity to express gratitude. What held you back, and how might you approach a similar situation differently in the future?

_____

_____

_____

_____

_____

_____

_____

_____

_____

_____

List three elements of the natural world you feel grateful for today (e.g., sunlight, clean air, or trees). How can you honor and reciprocate these gifts?

_____

_____

_____

_____

_____

_____

_____

_____

_____

_____

_____

Actionable Steps

1. **Gratitude Letter**: Write a letter to someone who has made a positive impact in your life. Share your appreciation with them directly, or keep it as a personal reflection.

2. **Daily Gratitude Practice**: Begin or end each day by noting three things you're grateful for, focusing on small, specific moments or experiences.

3. **Create a Gratitude Ritual**: Incorporate a simple ritual, such as giving thanks before meals or during nature walks, to regularly remind yourself of life's gifts.

"Gratitude is not only the greatest of virtues

but the parent of all the others."

— Cicero

Chapter 4: The Ethics of Giving and Receiving

Key Insights

- **Balanced Exchange**: True reciprocity exists when both giving and receiving are done with intention, respect, and awareness. It is not about equivalence but fostering relationships that benefit all parties.

- **The Moral Foundation of Reciprocity**: The ethics of giving and receiving call for recognizing and respecting the interconnectedness of life. This involves understanding that every gift, whether from nature or humans, carries responsibility.

- **Cultural Lessons from Reciprocity**: Indigenous wisdom teaches that gifts are part of a cycle, not a transaction. When we receive, we are obligated to pass something forward, ensuring the cycle continues.

- **Overcoming Self-Interest**: In a scarcity-driven society, receiving is often undervalued, and giving is viewed through the lens of sacrifice. Embracing reciprocity requires a shift from self-interest to mutual benefit.

- **The Risk of Imbalance**: When one side gives without receiving, or receives without giving back, relationships (and ecosystems) become strained. Ethical giving and receiving maintain harmony and equity.

- **Gifts in Nature as a Model**: The serviceberry tree exemplifies ethical exchange—it gives its fruit freely, ensuring survival for birds, animals, and humans, while benefiting from seed dispersal. This natural reciprocity fosters balance and abundance.

Reflective Exercises

Reflect on a time when you gave something without expecting anything in return. How did it make you feel, and what impact did it have on the recipient?

_____

_____

_____

_____

_____

_____

_____

_____

Think about a recent gift you received (tangible or intangible). How did you respond, and how can you honor that gift through your actions?

_____

_____

_____

_____

_____

_____

_____

_____

_____

_____

What barriers do you face when it comes to receiving
gifts or help from others? How might addressing these
barriers improve your relationships?

_____

_____

_____

• • •

_____

_____

_____

_____

_____

_____

_____

Consider an area in your life where you feel an imbalance in giving or receiving. What steps can you take to restore equilibrium?

_____

_____

_____

_____

_____

_____

_____

_____

_____

_____

Reflect on the idea of responsibility in receiving. How can you ensure that what you take is returned to others or the environment in some form?

_____

_____

_____

_____

_____

_____

_____

_____

_____

_____

Actionable Steps

1. **Create a Reciprocity Plan**: Choose one gift (time, knowledge, resources, etc.) you regularly receive and identify ways to give back to the source — whether it's a person, community, or nature.

2. **Practice Active Receiving**: The next time someone offers you a gift, help, or kindness, accept it with gratitude instead of hesitation. Reflect on how you can continue the cycle.

3. **Give Meaningfully**: Commit to giving something this week that aligns with the recipient's needs and values, ensuring your action creates genuine benefit.

"To give and receive are one in truth. No act of kindness is complete unless it inspires another."

— Inspired by Robin Wall Kimmerer

Chapter 5: Interconnected Communities: Flourishing Together

Key Insights

- **The Web of Interconnection**: Communities, like ecosystems, thrive on the principle of interdependence. Every individual plays a role, contributing to and benefiting from the collective.

- **Flourishing Through Collaboration**: Just as plants, animals, and fungi collaborate for survival, human communities are stronger when resources, knowledge, and care are shared.

- **The Role of Trust in Community**: Trust is the foundation of healthy, interconnected communities. It allows for vulnerability, reciprocity, and long-term relationships.

- **Learning from Nature's Communities**: From forests to coral reefs, nature demonstrates that thriving ecosystems depend on diverse members working together, each offering unique strengths.

- **The Danger of Isolation**: Communities weaken when individuals prioritize self-interest or withdraw from collaboration. Isolation disrupts the natural flow of support and shared growth.

- **Creating Flourishing Communities**: Flourishing requires intentional effort—listening, giving, and being open to receiving. It's about seeing ourselves as part of a larger whole and aligning our actions with communal well-being.

Reflective Exercises

Reflect on a community you are part of (e.g., family, work, or neighborhood). What do you contribute to its success, and what do you receive in return?

_____

_____

_____

_____

_____

_____

_____

_____

_____

Think of a time when your community worked together to solve a challenge or achieve a goal. What made it successful, and what lessons can you apply to other areas of your life?

_____

_____

_____

_____

_____

_____

_____

_____

Identify one area where your community could improve (e.g., communication, resource sharing, or trust). How can you personally contribute to this improvement?

_____

_____

_____

_____

_____

_____

_____

_____

_____

Consider your role in fostering diversity and inclusivity in your community. How do you create space for different voices and perspectives?

_____

_____

_____

_____

_____

_____

_____

_____

_____

Reflect on a moment when someone in your community supported you during a time of need. How did it shape your sense of belonging, and how can you pay it forward?

_____

_____

_____

_____

_____

_____

_____

_____

_____

_____

_____

Actionable Steps

1. **Strengthen Connections**: Reach out to a
   member of your community this week—
   whether a friend, neighbor, or colleague—and
   ask how you can support them.

2. **Build a Community Project**: Propose or join an
   initiative that benefits your group, such as

organizing a local clean-up, sharing resources, or planning a communal gathering.

3. **Foster Inclusivity**: Identify one way to create a more inclusive environment in your community. This might include amplifying underrepresented voices or welcoming new members.

"A community that flourishes is one where every member gives, receives, and grows. Just as the forest thrives through its connections, so do we."

— Inspired by Robin Wall Kimmerer

Chapter 6: Indigenous Wisdom: Respecting and Learning from the Land

Key Insights

- **The Land as Teacher**: Indigenous traditions view the land not as a resource to exploit but as a living teacher that offers wisdom and guidance through its cycles and relationships.

- **Reciprocity with the Earth**: The principle of giving back to the earth is central to Indigenous wisdom. This involves taking only what is needed, honoring what is received, and ensuring the land is cared for and regenerated.

- **Stories as Vessels of Knowledge**: Indigenous stories preserve ecological understanding, teaching us about sustainability, respect, and the interconnectedness of life. These narratives offer timeless lessons for modern challenges.

- **Living in Relationship**: Indigenous worldviews emphasize that humans are not separate from nature but part of its intricate web. Respecting this relationship fosters harmony and mutual flourishing.

- **Honoring Ancestral Practices**: Indigenous practices like seasonal harvesting, controlled burns, and sustainable agriculture demonstrate a deep understanding of ecological systems. These practices remind us of humanity's responsibility to live as stewards of the earth.

- **Rejecting Exploitation**: Modern economies often prioritize short-term gain over long-term sustainability, eroding the health of ecosystems. Indigenous wisdom offers a path back to balance, urging us to prioritize care and responsibility over extraction.

Reflective Exercises

Reflect on a time when you felt deeply connected to the land (e.g., during a walk in nature or while gardening). What did you learn from this experience?

_____

_____

_____

_____

_____

_____

_____

_____

_____

Consider the ways you interact with the natural world. Are there habits or practices you could change to honor the land more respectfully?

_____

_____

_____

_____

_____

_____

_____

_____

_____

Think about a story or tradition from your own culture that teaches respect for nature. How can you apply its lessons in your daily life?

_____

_____

_____

_____

_____

_____

_____

_____

_____

_____

Reflect on the concept of giving back to the land. What
does this mean to you, and how can you incorporate it
into your life (e.g., through planting, conserving
resources, or advocacy)?

_____

_____

_____

_____

_____

_____

_____

_____

_____

_____

Imagine a future where humans live in harmony with the earth. What steps can you take personally or within your community to move toward this vision?

_____

_____

_____

_____

_____

_____

_____

_____

————————————————————

————————————————————

————————————————————

Actionable Steps

1. **Learn and Share Stories**: Research an Indigenous story or practice that emphasizes respect for the land. Share what you've learned with friends or family to spark discussion about sustainability.

2. **Practice Land Reciprocity**: Commit to one act of reciprocity with the land, such as planting trees, composting, or supporting local conservation efforts.

3. **Reevaluate Consumption**: Examine your consumption habits and make a change to reduce your environmental footprint—whether it's minimizing waste, supporting sustainable products, or conserving water and energy.

"The earth is not just our environment. It is our community, our teacher, and our source of life. When we respect the land, we respect ourselves."

— Inspired by Robin Wall Kimmerer

Chapter 7: Reimagining Currencies: What Do You Truly Value?

Key Insights

- **Beyond Monetary Wealth**: Traditional economies prioritize monetary wealth, often overlooking the richness of relationships, knowledge, and shared experiences. True value lies in what enhances the quality of life for individuals and communities.

- **The Currency of Reciprocity**: In a gift economy, wealth is measured by what is given, not hoarded. Reciprocity creates a cycle of abundance where relationships, trust, and well-being are prioritized over material gain.

- **Redefining Success**: Success should be measured not by accumulation but by meaningful contributions to the world —

whether through kindness, creativity, or acts of service.

- **The Hidden Costs of Hoarding**: Hoarding disrupts the natural flow of resources, creating inequality and isolation. Giving freely fosters connection and ensures sustainability.

- **Aligning Value with Actions**: When we align what we truly value with how we spend our time, energy, and resources, we create a more fulfilling life.

- **Inspiration from Nature's Currencies**: Nature's "currencies" include sunlight, water, and nutrients—shared freely and distributed to ensure mutual flourishing. These principles remind us to create economies that serve collective well-being.

Reflective Exercises

Reflect on what you currently value most in your life (e.g., relationships, health, creativity). Are your daily actions aligned with these values? Why or why not?

_____

_____

_____

_____

_____

_____

_____

_____

Think of a time when you felt truly "wealthy" in a non-monetary sense (e.g., receiving help, sharing joy, or feeling deeply connected). What contributed to that feeling?

_____

_____

_____

_____

_____

_____

_____

_____

_____

What "currencies" do you bring to your relationships or community (e.g., time, empathy, knowledge)? How do you ensure they flow freely?

_____

_____

_____

_____

_____

_____

_____

_____

_____

Consider an area of your life where you feel stuck in a scarcity mindset (e.g., work, finances, or relationships). How can you reframe it to focus on abundance and sharing?

_____

_____

_____

_____

_____

_____

_____

_____

_____

_____

Reflect on how you spend your resources (time, money, energy). Are these expenditures aligned with what you truly value? What changes can you make?

_____

_____

_____

_____

_____

_____

_____

_____

_____

_____

_____

Actionable Steps

1. **Define Your True Wealth**: Write down three things you value most that aren't monetary. Reflect on how you can invest more in these areas daily or weekly.

2. **Practice Giving Freely**: Identify one "currency" you can share with someone in need (e.g., time, knowledge, or kindness) without expecting anything in return.

3. **Audit Your Spending**: Track how you spend your time, energy, and money for one week. Identify areas where your actions do not align with your values and set a plan to adjust.

"True wealth lies not in what we keep for ourselves but in what we give freely to others, knowing that the cycle of giving enriches us all."

— Inspired by Robin Wall Kimmerer

Chapter 8: Cultivating Generosity in a Competitive World

Key Insights

- **Generosity as Resistance**: In a world driven by competition and scarcity, generosity becomes a radical act. It challenges the fear-based mindset of hoarding and promotes trust, connection, and collaboration.

- **The Ripple Effect of Generosity**: A single act of generosity can inspire others, creating a chain reaction that transforms relationships and communities. Like seeds dispersed by the serviceberry tree, generosity fosters growth far beyond its initial act.

- **Generosity and Vulnerability**: True generosity requires vulnerability—opening oneself to give without guarantees of reciprocation. This trust is a cornerstone of reciprocal relationships.

- **The Competitive Trap**: Competition often isolates individuals and diminishes collaboration, reinforcing scarcity-driven behaviors. Generosity counters this by prioritizing collective well-being over individual gain.

- **The Joy of Giving**: Generosity is not just a benefit to others; it enriches the giver, fostering a sense of purpose, fulfillment, and deeper connections.

- **Practical Generosity**: Generosity is not limited to material gifts. Sharing time, attention, knowledge, or encouragement can create profound impact and cultivate a spirit of giving in others.

Reflective Exercises

Reflect on a time when you acted generously without expecting anything in return. How did it make you feel, and what impact did it have on the recipient?

_____

_____

_____

_____

_____

_____

_____

_____

_____

Consider a moment when someone's generosity made a difference in your life. How did their action affect your perspective on giving?

• • •

_____

_____

_____

_____

_____

_____

_____

_____

_____

What fears or barriers prevent you from being more generous? How can you overcome them?

_____

_____

_____

_____

_____

_____

_____

_____

_____

_____

Reflect on the competitive aspects of your personal or
professional life. How might generosity improve your
relationships and outcomes in these areas?

_____

_____

_____

_____

_____

_____

_____

_____

_____

_____

Identify three non-material ways you can practice generosity (e.g., offering time, listening, or sharing knowledge). How might these actions impact others and yourself?

_____

_____

_____

_____

_____

_____

_____

_____

_____

_____

Actionable Steps

1. **Create a Giving Plan**: Choose one area where you can intentionally practice generosity (e.g., helping a neighbor, mentoring someone, or donating resources). Make it a regular habit.

2. **Celebrate Others**: Identify someone in your life who often goes unrecognized for their efforts. Offer them encouragement, gratitude, or support to acknowledge their contribution.

3. **Pause Before Competing**: The next time you feel driven by competition, pause and consider how generosity could lead to a better outcome for everyone involved. Act on that insight.

"Generosity is the seed of abundance. When we give freely, we invite connection, trust, and the flourishing of all."

— Inspired by Robin Wall Kimmerer

Chapter 9: Harmony with the Earth: Reciprocity with Nature

Key Insights

- **Nature as a Partner**: Indigenous teachings view the earth not as a resource to exploit but as a partner in a reciprocal relationship. By taking only what we need and giving back in meaningful ways, we align ourselves with nature's rhythms.

- **The Principle of Reciprocity**: Reciprocity with nature means acknowledging the gifts we receive—air, water, food—and taking responsibility for replenishing and caring for the ecosystems that sustain us.

- **Mutual Flourishing**: The health of humans is tied directly to the health of the planet. Just as the serviceberry tree thrives by sharing its fruit, we thrive when we nurture and protect the natural world.

- **Recognizing Nature's Gifts**: Every interaction with the natural world is an opportunity to practice gratitude and stewardship. From clean water to shade from a tree, these gifts remind us of our dependence on the earth.

- **Living in Balance**: Modern lifestyles often disrupt ecological balance, leading to environmental degradation. Restoring harmony requires rethinking our consumption patterns and cultivating sustainable practices.

- **Learning from the Ecosystem**: Nature demonstrates the value of collaboration and shared resources. Observing and emulating these practices fosters a mindset of care and mutual respect.

Reflective Exercises

Reflect on a time when nature provided you with a profound sense of peace or healing. How can you honor that gift through your actions?

_____

_____

_____

_____

_____

_____

_____

_____

_____

Think of a natural resource you use daily (e.g., water, sunlight, or food). How can you reduce waste or give back to ensure its sustainability?

_____

_____

_____

_____

_____

_____

_____

_____

_____

Consider an area in your local environment that needs care or restoration. What steps can you take to contribute to its recovery?

_____

_____

_____

• • •

_____

_____

_____

_____

_____

_____

_____

Reflect on the gifts you receive from the earth (e.g., clean air, biodiversity, beauty). What specific actions can you take to reciprocate these gifts?

_____

_____

_____

_____

_____

_____

_____

_____

_____

_____

Imagine a future where humanity lives in harmony
with the earth. What role can you play in bringing this
vision closer to reality?

_____

_____

_____

_____

_____

_____

_____

_____

_____

Actionable Steps

1. **Adopt Sustainable Practices**: Choose one habit to adjust—such as reducing single-use plastics, conserving water, or planting native species— and make it part of your daily life.

2. **Participate in Environmental Efforts**: Join or support local initiatives focused on conservation, cleanup, or community gardens. Even small actions contribute to ecological harmony.

3. **Create a Nature Gratitude Ritual**: Spend time outdoors each week reflecting on the gifts nature provides, and take a deliberate action— such as picking up litter or watering plants—as an act of gratitude.

"The earth does not belong to us; we belong to the earth. To live in harmony with nature is to honor this truth through every choice we make."

— Inspired by Robin Wall Kimmerer

Chapter 10: Creating a Personal Reciprocity Plan

Key Insights

- **The Cycle of Reciprocity**: Living with reciprocity means creating a consistent flow of giving and receiving, not only in relationships but also with nature and community. A personal reciprocity plan formalizes this practice, making it intentional and actionable.

- **Aligning Actions with Values**: To craft a meaningful reciprocity plan, it's essential to identify what you value most and ensure your time, resources, and energy are directed toward nurturing those areas.

- **Sustainability Through Intentionality**: A well-thought-out plan ensures your acts of giving are sustainable, preventing burnout while fostering lasting, positive impacts on others and the environment.

- **The Ripple Effect**: When individuals commit to reciprocity, their actions inspire others, creating a collective shift toward generosity, trust, and shared well-being.

- **Measuring Success in Non-Material Ways**: A personal reciprocity plan focuses on intangible successes, such as strengthened relationships, community growth, and environmental stewardship, rather than material outcomes.

- **Adapting Over Time**: Reciprocity plans are living frameworks that evolve as needs, resources, and relationships change. Regular reflection and adjustment ensure continued relevance and impact.

Reflective Exercises

Reflect on the areas of your life where you feel most grateful (e.g., relationships, nature, or career). How can you give back in ways that honor those gifts?

_____

_____

_____

_____

_____

_____

_____

_____

_____

Think about the relationships in your life. Are there individuals or communities you've been taking more from than giving? How can you restore balance?

_____

_____

_____

_____

_____

_____

_____

_____

_____

Reflect on your environmental footprint. What steps can you take to reduce harm and contribute positively to the ecosystems you rely on?

_____

_____

_____

_____

_____

_____

_____

_____

_____

_____

Consider your professional or creative life. How can your skills or expertise be shared to benefit others without expectation of reward?

_____

_____

_____

_____

_____

_____

_____

_____

_____

_____

Imagine a year from now, reflecting on your reciprocity plan. What outcomes would make you feel that you lived in alignment with your values?

_____

_____

_____

_____

_____

_____

_____

_____

Actionable Steps

1. **Identify Key Areas of Reciprocity**: Choose three areas where you want to focus your reciprocity efforts (e.g., personal relationships, community, or environmental stewardship). Write down one specific action for each area.

2. **Set Measurable Goals**: Define what success looks like for your reciprocity plan. For example, "Volunteer twice a month," "Plant a garden for local pollinators," or "Regularly express gratitude to colleagues."

3. **Commit to Regular Reflection**: Schedule monthly or quarterly check-ins with yourself to review your progress, celebrate successes, and adjust your plan as needed.

"Reciprocity is the root of all thriving. When we give to the earth, to each other, and to ourselves, we create a cycle of abundance that sustains life itself."

— Inspired by Robin Wall Kimmerer

Final Self-Evaluation Questions

How has your understanding of abundance and reciprocity evolved throughout this workbook? In what ways can you apply these concepts to your daily life?

Reflect on a specific moment in your life when you practiced reciprocity. How did it impact your relationships, community, or connection to nature?

_____

_____

_____

_____

_____

_____

_____

_____

_____

What values have you identified as most important to you during this process, and how do they align with the principles of a gift economy?

How do you perceive your role within your community after completing this workbook? What specific steps can you take to contribute to its flourishing?

_____

_____

_____

_____

_____

_____

_____

_____

_____

Which practices from this workbook do you feel have had the most profound impact on your mindset, and why? How will you sustain these practices?

_____

_____

_____

_____

_____

_____

_____

_____

_____

Reflecting on the relationship between giving and receiving, what have you learned about balance and the ethics of reciprocity?

_____

_____

_____

_____

_____

_____

_____

_____

_____

What lessons from Indigenous wisdom and natural systems resonate most with you, and how do you plan to honor these teachings in your own life?

How has this workbook shifted your perspective on wealth and value? What aspects of your life do you now view as your greatest "currencies"?

_____

_____

_____

_____

_____

_____

_____

_____

_____

What challenges or obstacles do you foresee in implementing a reciprocity-focused approach in your life, and how might you overcome them?

_____

_____

_____

_____

_____

_____

_____

_____

_____

Imagine a world where reciprocity and abundance are the foundations of human interaction. What role do you envision yourself playing in creating this world?

_____

_____

_____

_____

_____

_____

_____

_____

_____

_____

The 30-Day Challenge: "Practical Application"

This 30-day challenge is designed to help you apply the principles of reciprocity, gratitude, and interconnectedness in your daily life. Each day includes a simple yet impactful action or reflection to foster personal growth, strengthen relationships, and deepen your connection to the natural world. You can journal your experiences and track your progress to make the most of this challenge.

Week 1: Gratitude and Awareness

Day 1: Write down three things you're grateful for today and why. Reflect on how they contribute to your sense of abundance.

Day 2: Spend 10 minutes observing a natural space (a tree, a garden, or even the sky). Note the gifts it provides to its environment.

Day 3: Express gratitude to someone who has impacted your life. Call, write, or thank them in person.

Day 4: Reflect on a time you received a gift (tangible or intangible) without expectation. How did it feel?

Day 5: Choose one item you no longer need and give it to someone who might benefit from it.

Day 6: Practice mindfulness with your meals today. Acknowledge the effort and resources that brought the food to your table.

Day 7: Journal about one area of your life where you often feel scarcity. How might you shift this to a mindset of abundance?

Week 2: Reciprocity in Action

Day 8: Perform a random act of kindness for someone without expecting anything in return.

Day 9: Spend 15 minutes cleaning up a natural area, such as picking up litter in a park or along a sidewalk.

Day 10: Share a piece of knowledge or a skill with someone who could benefit from it.

Day 11: Reflect on a relationship where the balance of giving and receiving feels off. What can you do to restore   harmony?

Day 12: Choose one habit that wastes resources (e.g., leaving lights on, wasting food). Commit to reducing it this   week.

Day 13: Spend time observing how an ecosystem (a garden, forest, or even insects) operates on reciprocity. What   lessons   can   you   apply?

Day 14: Identify a person, organization, or cause you admire. Consider how you can support their work— financially or through your time.

Week 3: Building Interconnection

Day 15: Reflect on the communities you're part of. Write down one way you can contribute more meaningfully   to   one   of   them.

Day 16: Spend time with someone from a different background or perspective. Listen actively to their story.

Day 17: Plant a tree, flowers, or herbs, or nurture a plant you already have. Reflect on how plants give back   to   their   environment.

Day 18: Offer encouragement or support to someone who seems to need it, even if they don't ask for it.

Day 19: Write down three non-material "currencies" you bring to your relationships (e.g., kindness, creativity, time).

Day 20: Reflect on your consumption habits for the day. What could you have done differently to use resources more mindfully?

Day 21: Host or organize a small gathering (virtual or in-person) to connect with friends or family. Focus on fostering meaningful conversations.

Week 4: Sustaining Reciprocity

Day 22: Commit to one long-term action that supports the earth (e.g., composting, reducing single-use plastics, or conserving water).

Day 23: Share a meal with someone and reflect together on the gifts of nature and the effort behind the food.

Day 24: Spend time reflecting on what you've learned about reciprocity. Write down three ways you've grown this month.

Day 25: Reach out to someone who may feel isolated. Offer your time and attention to brighten their day.

Day 26: Donate time, money, or resources to a cause that aligns with your values. Reflect on how this act aligns with your reciprocity plan.

Day 27: Write a thank-you note to yourself, acknowledging the effort you've put into growing through this challenge.

Day 28: Reflect on the natural world around you. How has your relationship with nature evolved over the past month?

Final Two Days: Integration

Day 29: Revisit your reflections and notes from this challenge. Identify key lessons and actions you want to carry forward.

Day 30: Create a personal reciprocity plan based on your journey over the last 30 days. Outline actionable steps you'll continue to practice in your life.

Made in the USA
Las Vegas, NV
18 December 2024

14595208R00056